Love is like a mutton chop
Sometimes warm and sometimes hot
Love is heavenly, love is strong
So is mutton if kept too long.

Love

is like a mutton chop...

Wry words of love 1840 - 1940

Collected by Beryl Peters

First published in Great Britain by
Copper Beech Publishing Ltd
© Copyright Beryl Peters 1993

ISBN 0 9516295 6 5

A CIP catalogue record for this book is available from the British Library.

Printed and bound in Great Britain

Copper Beech Publishing Ltd
P.O. Box 159, East Grinstead
Sussex RH19 4FS England

Women are like boots -
very useful, very desirable,
but a torment if you get a misfit.
1914

The wind, the wind, the wicked wind,
It blows the skirts knee high
The Lord was just, he sent the dust
To blind the bad man's eye.
1916

Man's a rebel, man's a rake,
Man was nature's sole mistake.
Man however well he may behave,
At his best he's only a monkey shaved!

1910

Mary had a little lamp
It was well trained no doubt
And every time the young man called
The little lamp went out.

1911

A kiss is a little side invention of the devil,
patented in Heaven.

1921

Man's love is like Dutch snuff
When you've had one pinch,
You've had enough!
1916

Lovers delight...................a lonely spot!
1919

Patience is a virtue,
Have it if you can.
Seldom found in woman
But never in a man.
1921

A youth of twenty summers
Wooed a maid of forty Junes
And the stars looked down at 1 am
On the latest thing in spoons.

1900

Little puffs of powder
Little dots of paint
Makes a girl's complexion
Look like what it ain't.

1919

My dearest darling turtle dove,
You are the one that I do love
If you love me as I love you,
Nothing but death shall part us two.

1910

Men, men, humbugging men,
You're impossible nine out of ten -
You're hopelessly mad things,
But still - "You're not bad things"
I do rather love you,
you men!

1911

Thou shalt not covet thy neighbour's wife,
Nor take his ox to slaughter,
But thanks to the saints it does not say
Thou shalt not covet his daughter.

1918

Under a shady tree they sat,
He held her hand, she held his hat,
He held that kissing was no crime,
She held her face up every time!

1914

Marriage Colours

Married in WHITE
you have chosen alright
Married in BLUE
you'll always be true
Married in RED
you'll wish yourself dead
Married in YELLOW
you're ashamed of the fellow
Married in BROWN
you'll live out of town
Married in PINK
your spirits will sink
Married in BLACK
you'll wish yourself back

1917

A woman's tongue is her sword
And she seldom allows it to rust!
1919

Two in a hammock trying to kiss
In less than a minute
They landed
Like This
1918

Here's to the man who kisses his wife
And kisses his wife alone
For there's many a man kisses another man's wife
When he ought to be kissing his own.

1921

A girl that has a kiss
And goes to tell her mother
Ought to be an old maid,
And never have another.

1918

Clifton is your name,
Single is your station
Pity the unlucky man
Who makes the alteration.

1925

All good girls love their brothers
But I so good have grown
As to love other girls' brothers
Far better than my own!
1916

The roses red, violet blue,
carnations sweet and so are you,
And so are they that send you this
And when we meet we'll have a kiss.
1913

Man wants but little here below,
And is not hard to please,
But woman, bless her little heart,
Wants everything she sees.
1895

HIS FIRST LOVE

A little boy to love inclined,
A little maid one day did find
Walking alone. He kept behind

like
this

Then to a seat at last came she
And she, being tired, sat down, you see
Right at the end; the other, he

like   this

At last he smiled and she smiled too
And soon the distance shorter grew
Between them as when lovers woo

likethis

But pa was passing by, and he
Dragged Tommy home and soon we see
That little boy on pater's knee

like this

1914

'Tis sweet to love
But oh how bitter
To love a girl
When her clothes don't fit her!
1917

King Solomon was the wisest man;
But keep from the girls he couldn't.
He loved them all, great and small,
And who the d... wouldn't?
1913

Although the cock croweth
The hen delivereth the goods.
1918

Many a shaft at random sent
Finds a mark the archer little meant.
1928

Here's to the happiest days of my life,
When I was in the arms of another man's wife
(my mother).
1917

When going through life, and you need an umbrella,
May it always be carried by a handsome young fellow.
1914

In golfing, you always
grip tightly with your left
hand, and your right hand
should rest lightly.

Arithmetic

He was teaching Eliza arithmetic
He said it was his mission
He kissed her once, he kissed her twice,
Then said, "Now that's addition".

And as they added smack to smack
In mutual satisfaction
He said now let us take a few more back
Then added "That's subtraction".

Then father came and raised his foot
And smiled in high derision
The chap struck earth three meadows off
And said "That's long division".

1915

Two's company,
Three's none
Four is alright
- if two will walk on.
1922

Sunshine and showers
Are alike to me
So long as you love me
And I love thee.
1916

Fall from a mountain
Fall from the heights above
Fall from the back of a donkey
But never fall in love.
1918

I wish I'd got someone to love me,
Someone to call me their own,
Someone to kiss and to cuddle me
For I'm tired of living alone.
1918

When this you see just think of me
tho' many miles apart,
Others shall have your company
but you shall have my heart.
1917

When first he came to meet her
'twas with a timid heart
And when the lights were low
They   sat   this   far   apart.

But as their love grew stronger
And they knew the joy of a kiss,
They knocked out all the spaces
Andsatascloseasthis.

1921

Be a good little girl
And let who will be naughty.
If you grow better day by day
How good you'll be at forty!
1914

Little drops of whisky
Little dabs of paint
Make a girl feel frisky
And feel like what she ain't.
1917

What gives to earth it's highest bliss,
I'm sure it is a little kiss,
I trust some day, my pretty miss,
That you'll not forget the words of this!
1915

From rocks and sands
and barren lands
May I preserved be.
And from great guns
and womens' tongues
Good Lord deliver me!

1916

❧

Be a good girl
Live a good life
Seek a good husband
And make a good wife.

1916

❧

Men are like fishes,
They would never get into trouble
If they kept their mouths shut.

1921

The ring is round, and so is the shilling
If you are ready, I am willing.
1916

The souls of women are so small;
That some believe they've none at all.
Lord Byron

I love every flower in your garden
One of them I longed to be
For I have seen you press them to your lips
Dear, if you would only care as much for me.

1915

Apples are ripe
Pears are better
If you love me true
Just answer my letter.
1916

Like the clinging ivy
Rooted firm and true
Strong and deep and tender
Are my thoughts of you.
1916

Tha struts abat like a brussel sprout
Tha thinks everybody loves thee,
But ah reet thee this to let thee know
Ah think misen above thee.
1890

What's in a Kiss?

There's something in a kiss,
Although you can't reveal it
It never comes amiss
Not even when you steal it.
1920

Women have many faults
Men have but two
There's nothing right they say
And nothing right they do.

1909

There was a young man of Perth
Who was born on the day of his birth.
He was married they said, on his wife's wedding day
And he died on his last day on earth.

1927

When Adam in bliss asked Eve for a kiss,
She puckered her lips with a coo,
And answered emphatic in words most ecstatic
I don't care a damn if I do.
1920

There's many a ship lost at sea
Through want of sail and rudder
And many a girl has lost her boy,
Through flirting with another.
1919

When you are near
The dullest day seems bright.
1919

WOMAN

There is not the slightest doubt
To a man she is a blessing.
Even though, year in year out,
All the while she keeps him guessing.
She is faithful, fond and fair,
Gentle, loving, kind and tender
Willing joy and grief to share
Gladly with her brave defender.
She was born to soothe and bless
Man may worship or command her;
But he may as well confess,
He will never understand her.

1915

Those who are wise, want love,
Those who love want wisdom.
1889

True love and ghosts
are both the same
Everyone talks about them
Few have seen them.
1895

Better trust all and be deceived
And weep that trust and that deceiving,
Than doubt one heart, which if believed
Had blest one's life with this believing.
1889

RECIPE FOR A WIFE

As much of beauty as presumes affection -
As much of cheerfulness as spurns dejection
Of modest diffidence, as claims protection;
A docile mind subservient to correction.
Yet, with sense, with reason, and reflection;
And every passion held in due subjection;
Just faults enough to keep her from perfection
Find this my friend and then make your selection.

1853

Love is like a war
easy to begin
hard to stop.
1890

Something rather naughty
Something rather nice,
Something rather wicked,
Though it can't be called a vice,
Some think it's saucy
Some think it wrong,
But all agree it's jolly
Though it won't last very long.
[A Kiss]
1930

What a conjure, what a cop
First you grow then you stop
Go to bis, earn quids,
Get married, have kids
What a conjure, what a cop.

1923

'Tis sweet to love
But oh how bitter
To love a girl
And then not get her!

1917

Advice

Put not your trust in women
Only in your mother
Girls, if you must love
Love one another.
Put not your trust in men,
Not even in your brother
Girls if you must love,
Love someone else's brother.
1910

God bless our wives
They fill our hives
With little bees and honey.
They sooth life's shocks
They mend men's socks
But don't they spend the money?
1916

A Romantic Love Story

They walked down the lane together
The night was full of stars,
He walked up to the gate with her
And lifted for her the bars.
She neither smiled nor thanked him,
Because she knew not how,
For he was only a farmer's lad,
And she was a Jersey cow!

1931

❧

If for me your love is true
Send me back my bow of blue.
If of me you sometimes think
Send me back my bow of pink.

1915

❧

They were in the parlour, just those three,
He, the parlour lamp and she.
Two is company without a doubt,
And so the little lamp went out.

1923

When the summer sun is setting
And your heart from care set free,
When of others you are thinking,
Will you sometimes think of me?

1917

You may fall from a church steeple
You may fall from heaven above
But the greatest fall you'll ever have
Is when you fall in love.

1920

LINES TO A SHORT LADY

I

When anything abounds, we find
That nobody will have it,
But when there's little of the kind,
Then every one doth crave it.

II

If wives are foils as 'tis known,
Some husbands, have confess'd,
The man who's wise will surely own
A little one is best.

III

The God of love's a little wight
But beautiful as thought,
Thou, too, art little, fair as light,
And every thing in <u>short.</u>

IV

Oh happy girl! I think thee so
For mark the poet's song -
"Man wants but little here below,
Nor wants that <u>little</u> long."
1840

Her smile was very sweet to see,
But ah! it wasn't meant for me.
How sad is life as on we jog -
That smile was wasted on a dog!
1916

Forget me not
Forget me never
Your love may change
But mine will never.
If separation be our lot,
Dearest heart
Forget me not.
1916

Just or Unjust?

Just a tiny path of moonlight,
Just a summer night in June
Just a hammock in a garden,
Just a dreamy distant tune.

Just a cuddly girl beside you,
Just an arm around her waist,
Just a pressure light of two lips,
Just a parting made in haste.

Why are lovers all molested,
Just at moments just like this?
Why are unjust people passing
Just in time to see that kiss?

1917

My heart is like a cabbage
It's nearly broke in two
The leaves I give to others,
The heart I give to you.

1899

There's nothing half so sweet in life
as love's young dream -
But in the summer "what ho!" ice cream!
1916

Why don't the men propose? 'Tis surely time!
I sit here gaily dressed; I trill my rhyme.
I sport like any school-girl, goodness knows,
I wonder why the fellahs don't propose?
1934

Read	I	love	find	you	you	will
up	that	you	I	love	for	be
and	see	if	if	me	love	for
down	will	you	but	not	my	got
and	you	love	me			

1938

Men are more eloquent than woman made,
But women are more powerful to persuade!
1929

Gone - And I always loved that girl so well!
Gone - Like the proberbial dear gazelle.
Or like the piece of toast so large and wide,
That always tumbles on the buttered side.

1920

When little girls tell tiny fibs
We turn all roary-tory,
And tell how lions ate the child
Who told one naughty story.
But when the girls adorn themselves
With hair-dye, paint and chignon,
They look so nice, that in a trice
We alter our opinion!

1928

A pretty girl, a crowded car,
"Please take my seat"
And there you are.
A crowded car, a woman plain,
She stands, and there you are again.
1926

God made parks
God made benches,
God made the little kids,
To kiss the little wenches!
1921

Man came into this world first,
His arm was made the strongest.
But to give a woman an equal chance,
Her tongue was made the longest.
1921

I know why they call girls 'peaches'
They've got lovely skins and stony hearts!

1920

∎

Oh, he who feeds the little pigs,
And gives the horses hay,
Have mercy on a little maid,
And send a lad this way!

1932

∎

When you are married and hubby gets cross,
Pick up the poker and say "I'm boss".

1921

He was dark and she was fair,
Sea-blue eyes and golden hair.
She placed herself upon a chair,
Now this is just what happened there.

He tried her on the sofa,
He tried her on a chair,
He tried her on the window sill
But could not do it there.

He tried her up against the wall
And standing on the floor
He tried her sitting on his lap
And by the parlour door.

He tried her this way and then that,
But how he made her laugh,
To see his patience as he tried
To take her photograph!

1921

48

What is Love?

Love it is a tickly thing
It drives you off your thatch
It makes you feel quite funny
In a place you cannot scratch

1921

Never make love in the cornfields
Remember the wheat has ears.

1914

When you are dead it is for a long time
But when you are married it is for ever.

1896

Oh! woman, loving patient woman
Best blessing in our house
So brave to bear the greatest pain,
Yet frightened by a mouse!

Oh! woman, fairest flower of earth
Since our race began,
Oh! be our love and angel still,
Don't try to be a man!
1909

THE PIANO LAMP

A lady had a birthday anniversary a short time ago, upon which her husband presented her with a pretty piano lamp. He was much flattered when she told him she intended giving it his name, until he asked her reasons for so peculiar a proceeding.

"Well," she answered, "you know dear, it has a good deal of brass about it, it is handsome to look at, it is not remarkably brilliant, requires a deal of attention, is sometimes unsteady on its legs, liable to explode when half full, flares up occasionally, is always out at bedtime and is bound to smoke!"

1907

A Shropshire Lad

When I was seventeen
I heard a wise man say,
'Give pounds and crowns and guineas,
But never your heart away.
Give pearls away and rubies,
But keep your fancy free.'
But I was only seventeen
No use to talk to me.

When I was one-and-twenty
I heard him say again,
The heart out of the bosom,
Is never given in vain,
'Tis paid with sighs a plenty,
And sold for endless rue,'
But I am two-and-twenty,
And oh! 'Tis true, 'tis true!

1933

Every man is a book
If you know how to read him.
1897

Cows like taters
Pigs like squash
I like you
I do by gosh!
1916

Man was made when nature was but an apprentice,
But woman when she was a skilful mistress of her art.
1921

HOW TO WIN
A GIRL'S HEART

A little bit of confidence
A little bit of zest,
Show a little willingness,
And she will do the rest.

Here's a little recipe
Sure to do it's duty
Telling how with little things,
To win a little beauty.

Get some merry thought
Get a little flour (flower)
Have a jolly little spoon,
And don't stir for an hour.

A little box of chocolate
A little bit of hare (hair)
A little touch of tender sole (soul)
A little bit of care.

Don't have many (k)nuts about,
Put them out of reach,
All the fruit that you require
Is just your little peach.

Warm things up with patience
Don't begin to press
And in a very little while
You'll get a little 'yes'.
1916

Cash governs the house that's the usual plan
Man governs the cash and baby governs the man,
Woman governs the baby and teaches it how to trot,
And when you come to reckon it up
It's woman who governs the lot.

1924

A man should wait til he is old enough
to get married
And when he is old enough,
He should know better.

1897

You talk about the age to wed
But really Miss, when all is said,
Let women while it's fine make hay
(As men get scarcer every day)
The age to wed? - just listen here -
Is when you have the chance my dear.

1909

My pen is bad, my ink is pale,
But my love for you shall never fail.

1915

A woman is never comfortable unless she is happy,
A man is never happy unless he is comfortable.

1910

Tulips - or - Twolips - which are the best?
Twolips are sweetest must be confessed
Tulips are pretty and gay to the eye
But Twolips when pressed 'electrify'.
1916

Without her leave he stole a kiss -
He did. Oh bliss!
A sharp command was promptly his;
"Just put that back, I tell you this,
Where it belongs," spoke haughty miss.
He did. Oh bliss!
1907

Love is like an onion,
You taste it with delight;
You wonder when you've eaten it
Whatever made you bite!
1919

The last in the book
I like to be,
But the last in your heart
Would be painful for me.
1933

*Copper Beech Gift Books
are designed and printed in the
United Kingdom.*